CAMEO

POEMS

BY

MELISSA DICKSON BLACKBURN

LCCN: 2010943215
ISBN 13: 978-0-9794561-3-8

Blackburn, Melissa Dickson
Cameo, Poems by Melissa Dickson Blackburn

Published by Summerfield Publishing,
New Plains Press
P.O. Box 1946
Auburn, AL 36831-1946
Newplainspress.com

The text of this book is composed in Garamond

Composition and cover design by Emily Wilkins

Cover Images:
Emilie Menzel by Adolph von Menzel, 1866
In the cameo, Union Survivor of Camp Sumter,
    Andersonville GA, 1865
    Library of Congress number: LC-USZC4-7966
Back cover author photo by FlipFlopFoto, Opelika, AL

I am indebted to many friends, poets, professionals, and mentors. Not the least of which are Dean Jackson, C. Scott Wilkerson, Johnny Summerfield, Denise Duhamel, Sarah Kennedy, Sue Walker, Alicia Clavell, Eve Stalker, Lan Lipscomb, Helen Silverstein, Jennifer Cooper, Catherine Moore, Johnna Flowers, Dr. J.R. Cooper, Tina Tatum at the Gnu's Room, and my classmates at Converse including Kathleen Nalley, J.R. Schrecongost, and Kate Kimbro. My sincere gratitude extends to each of you.

Grateful acknowledgement and appreciation to the following journals in which these poems originally appeared, sometimes in slightly altered forms:

Birmingham Arts Journal, "How to Raise a Girl Poet"

Breadcrumb Scabs, "My First Husband"

Driftwood Review, "I Wandered Like I Wandered Lonely," and "Coney Island" (as "It was the Baby")

Glass, a journal of Poetry, "Yellow Jackets"

Gnu Writers, "What is Mortal"

North American Review, "I Flew"

Shot Glass Journal, "On the Passing of Gourmet" (originally titled, "Bitter Sonnet") and "Mirror"

Southern Women's Review "If You Forget Me"

Thanks also to the Chattahoochee Valley Writer's Conference for acknowledging "Gran-dad Played the Trumpet."

For my father,

LT. COL. RICHARD G. DICKSON

1943-2006

Buried at Andersonville National Cemetery

and for those before him

CAMEO

CONTENTS

History is filled with the sound of silken slippers going downstairs and wooden shoes coming up.

—Voltaire

First Edition, 1924

The Lincoln Library of Essential Information
was my gift from Gran-dad's
barrister case. In my care,
its rear flank fled. Rubber-banded,
shackled, his book and I advanced
station to station. I gleaned
my bearings from its fathomless
frame: Schiller, Kant, the uneasy
ecstasy of thought, what we
own, what we know, and how long
we hold the things we receive.

BREAD RATION

for John Lewis Camp and his brothers
for my father and his brothers

Till I saw William, still as empty boots,
I took Chancellorsville grinning, day-dreaming
over Johnny cakes all the stories we'd tell:
how we bound ten Yankees, crying for home,
to Andersonville, and battled most the ache
for Mama's Sunday bread. Then Bob shook
and stopped dead on the long road to Richmond.
And imprisoned beside me, David burned
to bone. For a year, I swallowed the memory
of my brothers with every crumb of Elmira
hard tack. Then I forded Susquehanna,
Appomattox, Chattahoochee, thinking
about our Mama and what bread she'll break
when one of her four jumps the creek back home.

AMERICA

for Julia Frances Lewis, mother of Amanda America Dickson

Between seasons, nothing to sow,
so I cradled the lost bolls to fashion
an infant white as master, and swaddled
her in my apron. I paced the rows
singing like Mama does till my song
fell to the rhythm of his coming
hoof beats and he swung me to his mare
in one course pull; my doll feathered
the field, raw cotton again. If the gin
sowed seed back into the spun cloth,
that is what he did. His one saw tooth
spearing the weave of my body's soft
thread, the boll planted inside me
as white and round as a moon at harvest.

GEORGE MANOA HALL

1830-1864, Deceased at Camp Sumter, Andersonville, GA

Dear Wife, I write to you from inside
the stockade, my shelter stitched with laces
torn from my brothers' last boots. What I eat
shifts with larva amid rank scraps of fat.
I swallow water filthy with waste
from a spring they call Providence. My gums
soften; I count each of my teeth as they
drop in the sand where I sleep. I wear
the wind through August thunder, ride
my quiet song of delirium, and bathe
in each day's hundred deaths. I call
for you, and name you the sky. I nurse
the white worms of my undressed wounds
until they take their black cassocks and fly.

In the Portrait Gallery

The Dead of Antietam, Mathew B. Brady

They took my picture, Mama. You will
find me soon enough. Small comfort you will know,
to see me lean to the solid heart
of this oak as though picnicking, my brothers
off for a swim while I nap. The rest
of my tale is not one that will mend
a mother's core. How I slid in the snap
of battle, fruit of another son's harvest,
listened to the soul ripen in my flesh,
sleepier each moment until there was
only the long limb of your voice rustling
the thicket of men. In silence they came,
rendered me here to this crib where, Mama,
you will gather and cradle me away.

Bulb Garden, Arlington House

Mary Custis Lee

That fall I split the lilies,
brought some toward the porch,
and thought by spring I'd see
battalions burst yellow from my soil.

Now, I hear, the bodies crowd
right to the stair, unmarked currents.
Rivers of boys furrow the garden, part
even the roses under my chamber's bay.

They bloom in long light
multiplying spring to spring,
as many blossoms below
ground as above.

DELIVERED

My husband wrote from inside
the stockade, his pen a splinter
of bone, his tent a leaf of wool.
I knead my bread as once,
I needed him and shift
in my kitchen among the darkening
elm. This is all he had to say:
*the water is unclean, the food
foul.* He named the sky Rebecca
for the storm grey of my dry eyes,
for the rain that falls without want
of him, for the clouds that gather
like the hem of my velvet cloak,
and the trail I leave when going.

Clio, the muse of history, is as thoroughly infected with lies
as a street whore with syphilis.

~ Schopenhauer

DAUGHTERS OF THE REVOLUTION

To claim a title, Anna phones to ask if I've finished
the family tree, if I remember the name
of General David Dickson's son born 1783,
if I filed my D.A.R. application or even my U. D. of C.
I say, *No*. Then, admit, chagrined, I don't know
who can second a motion, or why our folks joined
the revolution only to abandon it in a new spin
on sovereignty, or what became of Mother
Nell's cameo, the cast iron commemoratives,
the tweed suit Grandmother wore to meetings.

But my boys are fine, and the Thai chili pepper plant
                    has plumped with hot fruit and, *yes*,

Dad would laugh if he saw us now, claiming
                    The Revolution as though it were our own.

WARRIOR COURT

We could see Stone Mountain from Grandmother's curb.
I knew Uncle David had conducted the novelty train
around its base; his authentic reproduction
Confederate uniform still hung, her spring dresses
parted around it, in the guest closet. So when I asked
Dad who won the war, and he pivoted my way,
not having to ask which war, and said, *They did,
the Yankees*, I confess, I was surprised. Stupid,
I suppose, to know only what was true on Warrior
Court. Stupid that it seemed absurd, but there she sat,
peacefully hearthside, drinking sweet vermouth
and watching Sarge at bat for the Braves
when we crossed the threshold and Dad whispered,
Don't mention it to Grandmother.

War Crimes

I am the one who stole the Nazi flag
from where it nested in the shadow
of Mother Nell's china kiln. Gran-dad pilfered
it from the battlefield, a soldier's right, not mine.
Like him, I wanted to study it, to know
it hanging over me, my dubious
headboard that sophomore year. I traced
its intricacies, proportions, black lines
knifing the red, an ancient Greek motif
of mitered rights, how art makes history,
what history makes of art. One starlit night
I escorted it past my chamber hold,
and the next, heaved it into a trench
beyond the dormitories' gravel yard.

THE GIRL WHOSE NAME
IS THE COLOR OF BLOOD

As God is my witness, I will not eat a fourth slice of pizza,
open that bag of Fritos, or break the fudgesicle's seal,
that's what Grandmother wanted to hear. *Hard,* she said,
to slide a Mammie-sized lass into Scarlet's corset. Pink and sassy,
I could sing *Hiawatha,* and quote the tale
of our ancestors' silver buckles stolen as Redcoats snaked
through Carolina. Even at 21 in a crew-cut,
bark cloth frock, and combat boots, I wanted her eye.
When I wondered out loud about the bell-curve
of my ass, when I threatened to date women and blacks,
I wanted still to be her prize. After we buried her,
I flew back to New York in a green-silk shift, up-do'ed
my chestnut hair and stunned a colleague from Seoul,
who shuddered past his shyness to ask

                  Do you know the one WITH THE WIND GONE?

GRAN-DAD PLAYED THE TRUMPET

and led an all-girl percussion ensemble called The Dixie Darlings

After they phoned to say he'd blown that end
note, we shimmied down the washboard roads
to witness Gran-dad's debut among the veteran
and Yankee dead. My uncle drove the hearse too fast
through Plains and by the time we struck Americus,
my cousin joked we'd ring President Jimmy
on the way back. When I heard that bugler falter, I
imagined Gran-dad shaking the head on his white
satin pillow, and saw him blow the brass mouth cold
against his own. While the rest of us whistled Dixie,
his casket like a timpani's skin trembled deeper
toward its vault. Then I got to rattle in the hearse,
right where Gran-dad had been, as the dirt
like a mallet tapped last on his grave.

DAUGHTER-IN-LAW

I saw Ann take two chicken breasts, one
for herself and the other for Jerry,
before I called anyone to dinner.
The only wishbone for ten children, she
pocketed for her own. When Jerry deployed,
Ann gleefully left for college. When he
came home—to her—faint with heroin and syphillis
she dared to send me notes. You'll find them
in that bin, left of Mother Nell's china hutch
with hundreds of carbon-copied letters
I wrote in my defense. I sent him every
antidote I could, a package each week
with snapshots of me, sharp razors,
Bazooka gum, his mother's coral kiss.

Yard Sale

Daddy said not to take less than forty,
but I let it go for twenty-five. Cheap,
I know, but my kids want this swing for Christmas,
one of those cedar types they've got at Sam's.
Daddy gave me a Brownie camera, and
a manual typewriter his Mama
used during the war, but this basket was
hardest to wrest from him. His daddy wove
it by firelight, a thousand bales rode
home in its hollow. Everybody wants
to know how I could sell it, but the truth
is, I don't pick cotton, and I can't think
of a reason I need to tote the chore
my grandfather set down sixty years ago.

Brinson's Race

for Laura

Saul Chance knew where Pop's wagon nested,
one axle rotten, the others leaning
westward. So when the new museum man
asked to buy it for his Americana Hall,
Saul said, *I'd sooner watch her turn to dirt.*
She'll stay where the last mule left her. That man
tried to say how it wasn't too late to
save Pop's wagon and the recollection
of those wood wheels turning against the field.
To which Saul replied, *I know where she is.*
And I remember fine my granddaddy
working the whip, the smell of that flogged
beast he loved. I'll die atop those hickory
planks, and the barn can yield to bury me.

1982 CADILLAC FLEETWOOD BROUGHAM

for Malcolm and Estelle

My papa worked the used lot at Weddington's
but Dean's dad, Malcolm, was shopping for new.
The leather-seated Brougham came in champagne
and burgundy, ten other lush shades. Malcolm
spied the platinum one and pondered its bright
digital displays flashing the details
in peacock blue. When Dean asked to drive it,
one spin of the old family farm was all
he got, heaving the weight of that Cadillac
through the empty fields his dad once plowed
by yoke and mule. Dean wanted him to set
the meters and test each gauge, but Malcolm
said, *No, I'm afraid if I ever look down,*
looking back up I'll see the ass of that mule.

On The Passing of *Gourmet*, November 2009

for Gail

It is the last issue of our *Gourmet*.
Here on the rim of winter, on the cusp
of consumption, how dare we foray
into seasons of culinary lust
sans our guide, sans brioche, sans cassoulet,
merry in the face of our dying delight,
minus the clear broth charm, the recipes,
the bread and wine of our gastric flights?
Tell me, dear, what meaty balm, what mastic
can seal this plunging and hungry absence?
Here is the turkey on page eighty-five,
bronzed, glazed, a poultry hallowed and divine.
Must we greet the year in bitter chagrin,
lovers of pages that won't roast again?

Historical sense and poetic sense should not, in the end, be contradictory, for if poetry is the little myth we make, history is the big myth we live, and in our living, constantly remake.

—Robert Penn Warren

LADDER

I should never have let him

name the beasts. A parent's first mistake

his worst, speaking as it will

to all the others. And then

that woman, one rung removed,

mounted each sound. His story,

I suppose. We all have

favorites, the shame's in saying so.

He was the best thing I ever did,

his syllables parted the air as I

could part the waves. And then

each word turned like clay

on her tongue until he believed

I meant to feed him my heart.

On Monsters

I can't say it without hearing the snicker of an old love,
my too long *uuu* and my *er* morphing into *aaahh*.
Naked was another word I learned to fear. Still, I will teach
my children the proper inflection. This morning over *nekid* eggs
and biscuits my son explained how *muhnstahs* form
under his bed, wrens with tiny wings and pumpkin heads,
allergic to lighting but drawn to electricity, in flight
as fast as a *crooked* (cricket). He plans to slay the naked
monsters struggling toward flight beneath his mattress
with string tied to an extension cord and a metal pole
I tore from my closet this morning, and I agree to give
my day digging shallow unmarked graves, a single sprig
of rosemary below the dirt, all the while singing,
as he does, *They grow up when they learn to eat you.*

Yellow Jackets

Here come my boys, chasing the late summer
breeze, screaming as they do every day, five
and seven years old, bickering for the best
blanket, or cap gun, or cherished cup. Today
their mouths stretch wider, searing grief labors
from each red throat. Both my sons bear cargos
of yellow jackets laced to their sleeves, cheeks,
one child's third striped eye hinged in rage and pain.
I strip and drench them, ice the welts and now
I fight alone, spray Lysol to slow the wings,
swing rags, hair brushes, my small bare palm—
dodging, stabbing at every flighted thing
while the hill of black and yellow dead swells
monumental, absolute, at my feet.

LUB-DUP

This is the sound of the heart, over half
is the sound of turning away, a door
slamming again and again, until the last
clap of valve against particle flow, the chamber
slowed to a vacuum lull. Picture the physician's ear
pressed tightly to a chest. A fire rustles
the patient's hearth. Wind whistles through a crack
in his cabin's pane. It is 1816, and soon
Laennec will turn on his lathe a dowel
of mahogany. Hollowed and capped with ivory,
it is the first proper stethoscope, ancestor
of the nickel-plated drum my son nuzzles
to my chest. He listens to the *yes*, the *no*, the *yes*
again and doesn't count each one, one less.

Coney Island, New York

It was the baby that always summoned me, not
the boardwalk, Nathan's hotdogs, the Cyclone
or even the ocean. It was the baby who watched
it all, swirling and visceral, wild gyrations of metal
and flesh, the length of our skirts, rising and falling,
and rising again. It was all a freak show. I, in its midst,
stood outside his jar, his red hair sprung up
in formaldehyde like the first sprigs of rye
in a newly seeded lawn, his nails too long, a century
since their only pruning. In a christening gown?
I can't recall. With a twin, a Siamese slightly smaller
fluttering face down? I stand still at his curb,
living and pushing toward death's glass
while he floats, cooing, *Come, the water's fine.*

I Wandered Like I Wandered Lonely

Amaryllis is a beautiful word
but it doesn't tell how red they are or
how they spread like motor oil, like lava,
in a WeeGee murder scene. It doesn't say
how to make them bloom again
or why they thrive in winter. Amaryllis
is a word and a bulb and a flower and a myth.

    I ran into a Pulitzer nominated poet at Wal-Mart today.
    He was picking up a re-issue of Nan Goldin's Ballad
    and I was returning Degas's Absinthe Drinker.
    I wanted to show him my white socks so like his own
    but there was a black hole dissolving my rib cage
    one rung at a time, there were children crying,
    there was an unmade bed in the parking lot.

How like the first blush of daffodil the absinthe blooms
How like war the embers crusade
How like Amaryllis the surge of each swallow
How like addiction the volcano's rampage
How like water the ash cascades
How like a bullet the sound of last call
How like Vesuvius the nights in Pompeii

In the pharmaceutical department a clerk restocks
Picasso's drunk, alone at his table and so like a clown.
Wild gyrations of crimson and chartreuse and wilder still
his eyes. Degas paints the man looking away, toward the bar,
and the woman in a gown the color of pale nectarine,
a spring bud limp at the table, her eyes a black fragment
of basalt, cold to the touch, already cast in plaster.

Bring Narcissus and his brittle beauty
Bring wild things that bloom by the highway
Bring girls in crinoline
Bring boys in costume
Bring rivers and linen and silver-dipped shells
Bring this, bring all you can hold
Tomorrow the volcano blows

Elegy for my New York

for Frank

With no more sound than the mouse
she was, I watch a mother move
her dozen youth. It is hot
under my claw-foot tub. She
cannot wait for me to bathe. She
follows the baseboard into my red
trimmed kitchen and nests behind a canister
that reads *This rice is wild.*
The mice are new, fresh from her basin.
She takes one at a time in her mouth.

       It took weeks to catch them all.
       One night I found three or four crying.
       The mother's body curled against the trap.
       Her open jaw stuck in glue.

My First Husband

For six years I boiled water,
soup pots to fill the bath,
the question of hot to cold
or cold to hot ever present.

For a while, we were happy,
climbing the loose stairs
of our tenement, stepping
lightly against the sway.

Paradise Lost

adamantine: Unbreakable (Gk.); C.P. Aeschylus's Prometheus, clamped "in shackles of binding adamant that cannot be broken" (*Prom 6*). The myth of adamant persists today. The indestructible claws of Marvel Comics hero Wolverine are made of "adamantium."
　　—*Paradise Lost,* Modern Classics Footnote

Wolverine with hands of adamantium here
you are heroic foot to Milton's note, page

fourteen of a Random House imprint. Adam writ
in clay and can we not say he was split, shattered.

His will like shist to her wit. Yet unbreakable, Adam
names your strength. And what of your heel

or the sole that bears your weight? What did
the Wolverine love? The fox in her velvet pillow,

a prism of light that fell from his eye. Oh marvel,
how man and woman came and came again.

How into being they be, unceremonious.
It's a nice day for a white wedding,

is from a tune by Billy Idol. By Jove, for love,
it should have been penned by Adam Ant.

Yellow Bicycle

after Robert Hass

If someone is reading this, we should tell them
it is a private conversation about a yellow bicycle.

I don't have ten dollars or a cigarette or a tube of coral
lipstick called *Pompeii at Dusk on the Eve of the Eruption.*

All I have is a yellow bicycle. Once I lived in a sea urchin shell
and then I gave it to a boy with a fig and a picture

of my yellow bicycle. The frescoes on the inside of my shell
are covered in cinder. The yellow bicycle has tires carved

from obsidian and spokes made of horse tail and hemlock
(lance-shape, sharp pointed, veins end at notches).

That's the thing about being born in a volcano, it's hard to see
your yellow bicycle. I could go on and on about the colors

and the pictures we painted but if you have ten dollars,we could
go buy donuts and lay them on the plaster casts at the museum.

BLUE FLOWER, BLACKBIRDS AT THE BUDDHIST TEMPLE OF GESSHOJI

If I slept with a boy because he reminded
me of the paintings we've seen of Shelley,
I know you will forgive me. Even at 18,
I was looking for that blue flower.

When we talk about the romantic poets
I'm not sure who we mean. Aren't they all
fatally romantic, pinned to each word
as blue to this frail flower?

I'm thinking of *Der Blaue Reiter* and how
Kandinsky's strokes cast the lone rider
in a blue cape, his blue shadow at the frame,
and a blue union of mountain and sky.

Every eye moves up and across the painting
from Prussian to ultra-marine and stops
at the horseman who clips the field, his white
steed's feet extended in cold air.

We used to think that painting abstract,
and now – hardly a wink at Yves Klein's
lapis lazuli monochromes. That's where we are,
and all I can think of is a blue hydrangea.

Somewhere in all this is a black bird borrowed
from Wallace Stevens but what I really want
is Albert Goldbarth's ruminations on the dead
Lizzie Rossetti underground with a manuscript

of her husband's unpublished poems pressed to her
own blue gown, ripe and velvet as the pomegranate
Proserpina fondles in Gabriel's portrait, her lips open
to speak, *Something will come of every grave.*

And here we fall into the grove of thirty-thousand
hydrangeas, where I have been going from the start,
toward the corpses in Japan silent as the blue
which blossoms again above them.

I Want You to Know One *Thang*

Alabama version after Neruda

the only lover I've ever sown knew not an anther
or leaf of me. He never held my Eastern Red Cedar
heart against his own of true cypress. He did not plunge
the midnight hollow of my plain or stroke the softness
of my limbs, the moon swell of my perimeter,
the secret shallows of my claim. He did not catalog
the humid reserves of endangered trillium, or brush
the jasmine cup of my shoulder or kiss the columbine
of my open lips. Not once did he explore tea olive arbors
or press his wrists against the flanked orchard of my chest.
No, his fingers never traced bright rosebud peaks, my tempered
cry against his cheeks. Never did he hold me, a garden
crowning fragrant around him or call my name into petaled
sheets or close my eyes in scented pleasure or in rooted sleep.

Special Offer

*If we ask, for instance, whether the position of the electron
remains the same, we must say "no"; if we ask whether the
electron's position changes with time, we must say "no"; if
we ask whether it is in motion, we must say "no."*
—J. Robert Oppenheimer

The ad claims to explain quantum mechanics
in three hours for less than seventy bucks.
When it's over I will know how the tiny
galaxies composing my beloved ping and snap,
sizzle inside the smeared margins of each
ever-fluxing atom. I will accept
what I cannot know: the speed at which
his love travels, and at that time, its distance
from my own. This is called uncertainty.
I will assemble all my tools to destroy
or preserve these principles. Eventually,
I will see, when he looks at me, I cease
to exist, still every miniscule and whipping
flame to measure the light in his eyes.

THE DANCE

This Grand Jeté   is not the one
she pictured.
This dance of the cat,   this side step,   this
    swagger

    isn't what   the choreographer had   in mind.
    He saw
a river bent   to brook.   He saw   a field of
    grackles

stopped mid-flight,   two hundred   maybe three
    all facing east, black   as abandoned silver.

This is how the ballet began,   the music
    unfamiliar, maybe   not yet written.

    Yes, there was a violin.   Though   she'd confess
a true love for wind.   Yes, there were
    long nights

    hunting stars   and birds on twinkling   limbs.
    You know
it all starts   and stops with the music,   the way
    the message
        enters
    the skin.
    Turn around,   ball step and slide.
She may dance   if music plays.
    She studied jazz.   She took ballet.   She
    knows how to
        tumble.

Mirror

There was a time she could not see
herself, alchemy of precious metal,
emplacement of eyes. Silver,
the mine of being, of having been.

The mine of being, of having been,
silver herself, alchemy of precious
metal, emplacement of eyes. There
was a time she could not see, herself.

NAMES OF BOYS

As poolside teens, my sister, Carrie,
and I tattooed the names of boys
onto our bronzing abdomens. On bright
white leaves we drew their names,
and trimmed each letter from the page.
We stenciled Dave, Scott, James,
ten other boys we claimed,
all month-long sweethearts that rarely
outlasted our tans. This was love,
as long as it stayed, a mark,
a stain, on a girl's transforming skin.

For A Stolen Stereo

Quietly he unfastened the latch, first
having tested dozens; the dark Windstars,
the sleek Saturns, all firmly locked against him.
Then my cherry coupe unbuttoned
at his touch. The glistening wires, breathless,
he revealed and unwound each cooper clasp.
Quickened and sure, his fingers pressed
the door into its mute frame and satisfied
with his soft touch, he drove my stereo away.
By morning light, only a tissue
blisters the drive and I feel him wipe
each trace clean, and smell the pall
of his hot breath, and hear the pitch
of night in which I soundly slept.

Parked Under A Crepe Myrtle At The Public Library

I recall my ex-husband's ex-girlfriend naming
them *Crepe Murder* for the way we prune
them tight, back to the trunk, after the fall,
so that they fill out, blooming like parasols
by summer. All spring the crepe myrtle
wear their truncated wounds,
startling as raw amputations, and every year
we do it again, passing the seasons this way:

wound,

     bloom,

          wound,

               bloom,

                    wound,

                         bloom.

It occurs to me, as perhaps it has to you,
that it is always this way; the wounding
and the blooming coming and going
in their course, so that we come to know it
as surely as we know our own waking
and sleeping, so that we fall into the light
and the dark without asking, anymore, why.

How To Raise A Girl-poet

The speed of light is very fast, carried by particles with
no rest mass. O'oo, that's weird.
—Rick Brantley, folk-singing mathematician

Next time your daughter asks,
                              Why is the sky blue?
Tell her,
           It's not. You think it is.

You will have told a truth.
                    The kind she needs to hear.

            No long tales of princesses
and fairies who hover in the glade.

Facts for your girl-poet.
            Let her know one particle
                              held still
                    has no measurable presence in this world.
            She needs to know there is no blue,

only things we call blue,

            for a moment.

THIS IS HOW THE FIG TREES

die back in September; the leaves curl in
on themselves like paper too long in sun.
Each leaf is a word I have forgotten.
The White Oak next door is the oldest tree
in the county. Rainwater collects
in its hollow. Our neighbors fear for us.
The children color my portrait outside.
I have three eyes, purple hair, an acorn
in my pocket. I know I decided
to forget. I forgot why, but I stopped
building the church with only the steeple
to go. I wanted, instead, to climb
that tree, to drink from its chasm, to eat
figs, and preserve what little I could.

LEOPARD PRINT PANTIES

I saw them first at a discount chain,
hung splendid and neat: cheetah, panther,
the rare painted lioness, forbidden plains
of sleeping fur, four legged and brutal.
The first pair, I took cautiously from the rack
and hid them in a din of kitchen crap.
Now, I spy them ruthlessly, a sniper
with one aim, my semainier shuffling
madly with skin, fur, and spotted pelt
of every unchained cat.

Hope is the other side of history.

—Marcia Cavell

ARMY CHILD RETURNS FROM GERMANY, 1976

They didn't know my grandparents had lived
on Buchanan Street since Papa got his first GI check.
I'd yet to learn my father's folks knew Peggy Mitchell
before *GONE WITH THE WIND*, and that my Scotch-Irish
ancestors fought Cornwallis in the Carolinas.
So when the first word any child said to me
was *Nazi*, I tried to explain I just came back home.
I didn't mention I'd already memorized five addresses,
lost my best friends, one by one, to new tours of duty,
and unpacked the box labeled dolls only to find
my favorite decapitated. It was the bicentennial.
Like the other girls I wore red, white, and blue,
but when my new teacher handed me a bottle of Coke
to slide inside the time capsule, I said, *Danke, Liebchen,*
like I meant it, and curtsied in my revolting red skirt.

COMBAT

Dean was nine by then, his brother
and I, just eight. I lived those years
a block away. The only game we knew
was war, waged relentlessly
in the boy's backyard, a no-man's land
of privet and invasive bamboo. I knew
to dig in past the drainage ditch, to find
a good stick, as big as theirs. I saved
my skirts for Sunday when the combat burned
fiercest, besieged by my mother's mother's
tyranny, my dress too long or too short,
the olive bruises on my shins too fresh,
and not once could I wear Papa's boots
beyond the enclave of her kitchen's hold.

CAMP SUMTER

Andersonville National Prisoner of War Museum

My father once said he'd leave me there, locked
inside the replica stockade. I'd asked
too many questions and wanted to know
more than he could kindly say. My uncles
all laughed. One gently offered to fashion
an impromptu shelter. Another reached
in his coat for a roll of Lifesavers
to lend. Grandmother pointed again
to the Deadzone rail and reminded me
not to cross it or a boy, no older
than I, would gun me down with a carbine
he could barely steady against his hip.
When I started to weep, my father sighed,
but marched on toward the car.

CEASEFIRE

You sound like cannon balls on the stairs,
Dad said. I forgot to ask what kind: heads
of Turkish captives fired from *falconet,*
an arrow blown from the *pot-de-fer,*
the federal quilted grape. He knew
the mid-century Howitzer best and when
he heard me running the basement steps,
a Confederate escaping the Union advance
of my older male cousins, he bolted
the upstairs latch, retreated to the den
and hollered another of his many
war metaphors, my feet heavy as his
brow, my body a quiescent artillery,
his last projectile stopped in flight.

I Flew

I flew with him once in a twin engine,
my father, the pilot. Anna and I
were fastened safely in the rear when Dad
turned, and waved me to his knee. I was nine,
Anna four. It was one joy I recall, teetering
fat on my father's lap, slung through air,
his right hand loose on my hip. I wish I
could say I sat there a long while as our
country knitted and unknitted beneath us,
but one engine quit and we fell what seemed
a tower's story. He swept me away.
A soldier again, his eyes patrolled the dash.
On my knees, my heart low on fuel, I knew
the best he could do was save our lives.

WE WERE ELEVEN

And tired of playing war when Dean pierced
the worn flank of his mother's hope chest
with the pistol his father kept bedside.
I could say I heard the shot from my room
around the bend, but what I heard was the story
of his mother's face, pale as the north star
at daybreak. Later another boy chased me
around a pedestal table with the .38 Special
harbored in his mother's sideboard. Now Dean
locks a semi-automatic in the chifforobe
and his mother's heart pine chest is plugged with oak,
and from our kitchen window, we cannot say
the difference in the fig tree he brought from his
grandmother's home and the one I brought from mine.

DEMILITARIZED ZONE, SEOUL

Dad worked the DMZ, ate kimchee
for a year. We dreamed he paced that seam
in fatigues, an M-40 tight to his chest.
In truth, he rode a desk, office jock
for Uncle Sam. We wanted to know
two things: what was the big deal between
the north and south (why the boys, lips pinched,
tracked the line, day after day), and if
he liked the kimchee, ubiquitous sheet
pulled pungent over Korea. He wouldn't
say, but after he came home, every time he
passed a garbage can left too long, he thought
of them, their cabbage rotting underground,
the little women who talked so fast.

Custom

In Korea, a man could have anything
custom stitched to order. That year,
Dad asked my desire, and I drew
for him a blouse with puffy sleeves
and a raised ruffle collar, said I
wanted it in rose rubbed cotton,
the slacks to match in hunter green
because it was 1980 and preppy
was in. Mom mailed my design
with his gifts and my late November
measurements. By April, my clothes arrived
without a note, just as I drew them,
beautiful with a sheen like polished stone,
already a size too small.

WHEN MY FATHER'S EYES OPENED
WE RAN FOR THE NURSE

My sister, Anna; Carol, the woman we loved,
and loved to call our mother; and I startled
from his bedside when his dark eyes ruptured
loose from that half-place, that not-living ellipsis
where his libretto was still being penned,
his finale, opulent, echoing
through the hospital corridor. Stupid.
Stupid women. You've bought your ticket.
You've pocketed the stub. This is not the time
to run. This is the scene you watched for,
the reason you came: the purple mottled toes,
the epic rattle, last neurons flicking
on a darkened stage, one slow tone, a muscle twitch,
no curtain call. Bravo, Daddy. Well done.

LOSING THE MOON

for Hurst Peacock and our fathers

My friend said losing his father was like
losing the moon, the eve ever present,
true as his own pale face, his bathroom sink,
the curve of his thumb nail. I want to see
my collarbone unsheathed from its thin sheet.
I want to know how true it is, how like the moon,
or the porcelain of bisque figurines.
Is it the white of bone china, of teeth,
of sea foam or milk, bright as the shirt
in which my father lies, or luminous
as headlamps in oncoming traffic? We have light
to measure every hue. In my kitchen, I force
the Paperwhites to bloom, to summon as
the seasons pass some shade of my lost moon.

Renovation

After you paint his house, its hundred windows,
balustrades, and fine original moldings, hire a man
in a weathered t-shirt that reads, *Do I look like
your therapist?* Ask him his address. If he knows it,
send him there. If he replies he's only here
a moment, visiting an ailing aunt or dropping
a friend along the way, task him with the chore
you cannot do yourself. Hand him the knife winnowed
with wear. Let him erase every hint of *Teal Mist*.
Instruct him to leave no trace of *Merry Melon* wedged
in the mullions, no *Rose Rumor* tainting the glaze.
Pay him well from your father's coin collection. Every
wheat penny, every verdigris nickel, and finally,
the midnight blue dime he bought on his 50th birthday.

WHAT IS MORTAL WILL BE SWALLOWED BY LIFE

1 Corinthians 15:54

as tea, as each moment in each room, and each
sun setting westward—swallowed. So the living
live and the dead are consumed, vapor trails,
smoke of the snuffed candle, the inverse burn
of light behind the closed lid. Order another
round, and drink till there is no more. No more
water. No more tea. No more wine. Each ounce
is one ounce more and, we can agree,
one ounce less. You are here, this dot
on this page. You are the bread broken,
the marigold unfolding its velum petals.
You are the wave as it breaks on the shore
and the particle that filters upward
through a slant of light in the open door.

CROSSING BLOOD MOUNTAIN

On the way to Young Harris, Dean says
it was the war between the Creek

and Cherokee that ran the mountain red,
a territorial dispute, a matter of expansion.

We are grown now and I want to walk the stone
chapel walls where my grandparents

worshipped, where Gran-daddy played
his trumpet and won the Golden Glove,

where Grandmother wore ermine collars
and memorized a lifetime of Longfellow.

We stop to sample wine at Crane Creek
and Three Wolves and by the time

we cross the campus gates,
the sun has set golden past the vineyards

and I am as soft as the grape's new leaves,
a child again, on the day of Uncle David's wedding,

hiding his bright military insignia
in Grandmother's jewelry safe. And now

I see it's not the war between us
she's left, but the pages stunned with poems,

all of them she knew, word for word,
and sings, still and again, to me.

History is an angel being blown backwards into the future...
and the angel wants to go back and fix things, to repair
the things that have been broken...
—Laurie Anderson

NOTES

During the writing and re-writing of Cameo, I struggled with
ideas of authenticity and ownership. In order to reconcile those issues
to my own satisfaction, I am including a few notes on the poems
which provide additional information, historical context, and, where
possible, acknowledge the original source of the story or idea. Any
factual errors are my own.

Bread Ration

John Lewis Camp was a confederate soldier and ancestor of Nelle
Camp, my father's grandmother, referred to in the collection as "Moth-
er Nell." John Lewis Camp survived the battle of Chancellorsville, a
great victory for the Confederacy, only to be captured and imprisoned
at Elmira POW Camp. His brothers did not survive the war. In the
poem I give him three brothers and name them after my father's three
brothers. My father and his brothers all served in the Army or Air
Force during periods of war and all survived. The younger brothers,
Richard and David, have both since died of cancer and are buried with
their parents in Andersonville. I was told about John Lewis Camp by
my Uncle Bill on the way to Uncle David's funeral at Andersonville.

America

Amanda America Dickson was the daughter of Julia Frances Lewis
and David Dickson. Lewis was a slave who belonged to Dickson's
household. Though he had raped Julia, Dickson remained loyal to
both mother and daughter and left his estate to Amanda. She became

the wealthiest black woman in the South despite the outcries of her white relatives. Her story is celebrated in Kent Anderson Leslie's biography, WOMAN OF COLOR, DAUGHTER OF PRIVILEGE: AMANDA AMERICA DICKSON, 1849-1893, and the Showtime Original Movie, *A House Divided*. I learned of her existence just before the publication of CAMEO and added this as a final poem. Our family lines converge in the mid to late 18th century in Halifax, Virginia.

George Manoa Hall

George Manoa Hall was the direct ancestor of my step-mother, Carol Ann Cook. While my father's ancestor John Lewis Camp was imprisoned at Elmira POW Camp in New York, Carol's ancestor died at Andersonville. He is buried near my father. I read a description of conditions at Andersonville in which a prisoner explains that there were no medical supplies to bind or protect injuries, and he had watched maggots become flies in his own wounds.

In The Portrait Gallery

Photographer Mathew Brady was one of the earliest photojournalists. His documentation of the Civil War was his greatest achievement. Brady hired a number of photographers to assist with the work including Alexander Gardner, T. H. O'Sullivan, and John Reekie. While Brady wanted to accurately reflect the war, evidence indicates that he moved bodies and staged scenes in order to create more dramatic photos.

Bulb Garden, Arlington House

The Custis-Lee Home was usurped from the Lee family for non-payment of taxes. While the family had sent a nephew with the funds, the payment was refused on the grounds that they had to be paid by the property owner in person. Robert E. Lee was at war, and travel of that kind was ill-advised for Mary Custis Lee. After claiming the property, Lincoln quickly ordered the burial of Union dead with the suggestion that they get as close to the house as possible. Ironically, the home is on land bequeathed to Mary Custis Lee by her father, the adopted son of

George Washington. I read this account in Wayne Youngblood and Ray Bond's photo book *MATHEW B. BRADY, AMERICA'S FIRST GREAT PHOTOGRAPHER*.

Gran-dad Played the Trumpet

This is the true story of my perspective of my grandfather's funeral. He was a retired Lt. Colonel who during World War Two coordinated USO shows. It is true that he had an all female percussion ensemble called *The Dixie Darlings* which included my grandmother's sister, Helen Copelan.

Mother-In-Law

This poem is based on a conversation my grandmother and I had when I was around 10 years-old. While she loved her sons ruthlessly, she had little patience with some of her daughters-in law. The first line is taken from one of the carbon-copied letters she instructed me to read during that conversation; the rest is invented.

Yard Sale

Is based on a conversation I overheard at a flea market in November 2010.

Brinson's Race

Robert Lane Overstreet told me this story about his cousin, Saul Chance. In the poem I imply that it was a mule drawn wagon to provide a connection to the mule in 1982 Fleetwood Brougham Cadillac. In fact, it was a fine, horse drawn carriage that was widely admired in the community. Saul Chance was the mix race descendent of Overstreet's Grandfather and his former slave, Pharabe Chance who is buried in the family cemetery at Brinson's Race.

1982 Cadillac Brougham

Dean told me this story about his father's Cadillac which he purchased when Dean was 15. At that time, my grandfather managed the used car lot at the dealership, Weddington's Chevrolet-Oldsmobile in Newnan, Georgia.

On the Passing of Gourmet Magazine

Gourmet Magazine published its last issue in November 2009.

Lub-dup

French physician René Laennec invented the stethoscope in 1816. His first prototypes were made of mahogany.

Coney Island, New York

The Coney Island Side Show used to feature an infant on display in a large laboratory jar. The exhibit had been part of the attraction for decades, perhaps since the amusements first opened in the late 1800s. It was a fairly common practice to feature human oddities, dead or alive, in amusement sideshows.

Camp Sumter, 1980

Andersonville National Cemetery was the location of the Confederate POW camp, Camp Sumter, infamous for overcrowding and death. According to the park's website, 40% of the Union POWs who died during the war, died at Camp Sumter. There is now a museum on the site and the original grounds of the POW Camp have been restored with a replica stockade and examples of the shelters which the men fashioned from available materials.

Demilitarized Zone, Seoul

My father was stationed at the DMZ in Seoul for one year. Anna, Carol, and I remained in Alabama.

When My Father's Eyes Opened

In a small percentage of deaths, the eyes will open as a result of muscle response to involuntary stimuli. We wanted to believe he was coming back, not that he had died.

What is Mortal Will be Swallowed by Life

This interpretation of the passage from Corinthians was used at my Uncle David's funeral just before his burial at Andersonville.

Melissa Dickson Blackburn

is a mother of three, Anna Frances, Reeves, and Brinson. She holds a BFA (Auburn University, AL) and MFA (School of Visual Arts, NY) in studio art. During the composition of Cameo she was completing an MFA in creative writing at Converse College, SC. As an undergraduate at Auburn University, she received the American Academy of Poets award. Her work has appeared in Southern Humanities Review, Caesura, Southern Women's Review, The Birmingham Arts Journal, Driftwood Review, Shot Glass Journal, and Breadcrumb Scabs. As a visual artist her work has been reviewed and acknowledged in The New Yorker, New York Magazine and The New York Times. Her first marriage to composer Frank J. Oteri was a performance art event based on Margaret Atwood poems and was covered by the New York Times. After a friendship of 35 years, she is happily engaged to Dean Jackson and eating figs with him in the backyard where they played war as children.

www.ingramcontent.com/pod-product-compliance
Lightning Source LLC
Chambersburg PA
CBHW031147090426
42738CB00008B/1247